From the Heart of a Mother

From the Heart of a Mother

by
Ruby E. Johnson

MOODY PRESS
CHICAGO

All Scripture quotations, except those noted otherwise, are from the *New American Standard Bible,* © 1960, 1962, 1963, 1968, 1971, 1972, 1973, 1975, and 1977 by The Lockman Foundation, and are used by permission.

Library of Congress Cataloging in Publication Data

Johnson, Ruby E.
    From the heart of a mother.

    1. Johnson, Ruby E. 2. Mothers—Religious
life. 3. Christian biography—United States.
I. Title.
BR1725.J625A34   1982   248.8:431:0924 [B] 82-8218
ISBN 0-8024-5090-3

Printed in the United States of America

Contents

Preface

It was a beautiful, sunny, crisp, January day, the last of the holiday season. Janet, Kent, and Curt had all been home, but now, as sun dogs frisked the sun into place below the horizon, I was delivering each one to his or her college dormitory.

We had enjoyed such a delightful two weeks that I hated to see it end, although I knew that it must. In fact, I really wouldn't have wanted it to be different, for I wanted them to be educated. Nevertheless, my feelings were ambivalent—a twinge of pain, perhaps, that accompanied their absence, but a definite twinkle of joy in their progress.

It was dark when I returned home. Minutes

before, my house had been throbbing with the sounds of youthful chatter and activity; now it was hollow with emptiness. The contrast was dramatic. The rhythmic ticktock of the kitchen clock could be heard clearly as it pricked the silence, a sound unheard when the family was at home. Slumping into an overstuffed chair, I tried to sort out my thoughts.

No masculine voices asked, "What're we having for supper, Ma?" or, "Where's my blue sock?" There were no girlish giggles, youthful banter, or friendly jostling—just deafening silence. In the space of a few minutes, I had to adjust from the extremes of an atmosphere that was at times too noisy to one that was much too quiet. It wasn't easy. Reliving the events of the past two weeks, I began to reminisce about the highlights of earlier years. What an array of adjustments!

That is when it hit me. Being a mother involves all kinds of adjustments. It occurred to me that *Ma* must be an abbreviation for *major adjustment* or *minor adjustment*. A mother's life is packed with them—adjustments of all kinds. When one hears the cry, "Ma!" it means, "Mother, brace yourself; here comes another adjustment, and it might be a biggie."

The ability to adapt to every adjustment and change in marriage and child-rearing—all the while remaining mentally healthy—is an enormous asset. God never intended that we should tackle the job alone, however. When He ordained marriage and the family, He wanted us to depend upon His resources for our success.

My husband and I discovered that we could not establish and maintain our family relationships successfully alone. We did not possess the qualities required for that kind of commitment. So we asked the Creator to help us. Without His guidance and assistance, we would have failed miserably.

This book will give you a glimpse into the lives of our family members and show how we coped with the problems we faced. Your problems may be different, but the principles will be the same. By sharing our problems. we trust you will find help in yours.

My "Ma" Degree

1

My "Ma" Degree

After the year-end holidays, near bedlam turned to near boredom as I sat alone in the living room staring at a blank television screen. What an array of adjustments life had handed me!

Sorting through the perplexities as they appeared on the screen of my memory, I decided that sitting alone in my house was not the most serious adjustment a person might face. On a scale of one to ten, that would have to be near the bottom, whereas having my first child might well top the list. He was an adjustment of major proportions.

First, I had to adjust to a different figure. Changing from lithe to lumpy in a few months' time had its rewards, however. It meant buying a new wardrobe of dresses and skirts, some of them attractive in spite of their beach ball cutouts.

But as time passed, my walk became a waddle,

and I could no longer tie my sneakers or pick up an object from the floor. Such clumsiness seemed ridiculous. There had to be an easier way to produce babies.

Then, just about the time I decided that laplessness was really quite funny and the other inconveniences a source of humor—whammo!—it was all over. Suddenly I was lithe again, and my tummy no longer thumped. Skip lay in his crib.

At his birth, I heard "Ma" for the first time. It really sounded more like "Wa," but that was because my baby was hanging by his feet and the doctor was paddling him. But then, W's are just M's hanging upside down. No matter how it sounded, that cry was my initiation into motherhood and its accompanying adjustments. My next one was not long in coming.

All the babies I had seen in magazines had been described as adorable and beautiful. I could hardly wait to get a glimpse of mine. He surely would be so appealing that even those adjectives would be inadequate to describe him properly. He had to be very special; he belonged to me and the man I loved dearly.

When my tiny blanketed bundle was placed in my arms and I saw him for the first time, I discovered he was indeed very special. Beautiful or adorable he was not. In fact, he did not look at all like the magazine pictures I had been gazing upon during those long months of waiting. The questions began to multiply.

Why was he so red? Why didn't he have eyes instead of watery slits? Where was his curly hair? No, he certainly was not a pretty baby. Most of his nursery mates were red too, and some even wore scruffy wigs, so they were not any prettier than Skip. Seeing them helped, and I decided that no newborn baby resembles those being advertised.

But Skip's appearance was not the greatest of my concerns as I held him in my arms for the first time. Other mothers with their babies appeared almost to fuse into one loving bundle as they held their tiny offspring. Not so with me. Even holding mine, I felt clumsy and awkward. Shifting him gingerly from one side to the other, I expected with each shift to be more at ease. But that did not help. I just didn't know how to hold him. A real mother with my own precious bundle of life, yet I wasn't comfortable with him. What could I do?

Even that failure was not my worst. Not only was I clumsy, I felt guilty too—guilty because I did not even love my baby (though I didn't dare tell a soul). I held him, gazed into his tiny face, analyzed his features, felt his warmth, but felt no love at all. He could have been a rag doll considering all the emotion I had for him.

Don't mothers always love their babies? Where were my motherly qualities? What was wrong with me? Poor Skip; he did not ask to be born. An innocent victim, he was completely helpless. He needed a mother's love so desperately. The more I thought about the dreadful state of affairs, the more depressed I became. Finally I collapsed in tears.

After we brought Skip home from the hospital, we discovered he was not only unattractive but inconsiderate as well. Though I did everything I could to keep him happy, my efforts seemed useless. He cried or screamed both day and night no matter what I did, until he fell asleep from sheer exhaustion.

Then Walt and I dropped into bed even more exhausted, only to be awakened a few minutes later by more crying. For months he disrupted every day's schedule and every night's rest until we became so unnerved that I feared we would fall apart.

Skip was not at all considerate, but I was learning what *Ma* is all about—adjustments and more adjustments. Each day had its share of crying spells; some were Skip's, some mine.

When Walt returned from work, we weren't a very pleasant twosome. Much of my depression stemmed from guilt for not loving my child. Had I shared my problem with my husband, I would have felt better about it, but I was afraid of his reaction. Already I was condemning myself, and I could not bear his possible condemnation too. My guilt had to be my secret—mine and God's, for I told Him all about it.

Then one day when Skip was about two months old, I was cradling him in my arms to nurse him.

His tiny fingers grasped my thumb and clutched firmly. There was nothing unusual about that, for he always held my thumb. Snuggling him with one arm, I guided the nipple to his eager lips. He seized it, and for the next twenty minutes or so he gulped contentedly.

As I watched, something unusual began to stir within me—something I had never before experienced. Cuddling Skip more closely, I admired his perfect features. Something was happening, for I felt a new kind of warmth evolving. As he continued to gulp, I squeezed him gently, and then I felt as though my heart would burst within me.

A new kind of love—mother love—came over me. Smiling with joy, I cuddled him again. What a peace overwhelmed me when I realized that at last I was a normal mother who loved her baby like other mothers loved theirs. No longer must I hide my guilt. I loved Skip with a genuine love.

The truth soon became evident that a mother's love is different from the kind of love my husband and I enjoyed, for our love was reciprocal. It is a cozy give-a-little but get-a-lot-more kind of relationship. A reciprocal love had been the only kind of love I had ever known.

Had Walt not been kind, generous, and considerate to me, it is likely I never would have cared for him at all, much less loved him. And Walt must have felt the same way about me.

But there was nothing reciprocal about my love for Skip. All the giving, cuddling, caring, loving came from me. Ours was almost a slave/master kind of relationship, with me as the slave.

Now that I loved him so much, I did not mind being his slave anymore. He remained selfish and self-centered, concerned only for his own well-being, with never a thought for mine. He did nothing to warrant love from me or from anybody else, and yet I loved him. Such a different kind of love was hard to grasp.

One day while I snuggled him, a new realization struck me. My one-sided love for my son was a sample, in miniature, of God's love for me. His love is even more one-sided than any mother's affection.

Skip eventually grew up and matured to become a very considerate, loving son who is deeply concerned about my needs. He now returns my love. "But God demonstrates His love toward us, in that while we were yet sinners, Christ died for us" (Romans 5:8).

God loved me when I was selfish, inconsiderate, and hateful, before I had any desire at all to please Him. That love would have continued even though it was not reciprocated. I am not sure of my continuing love for Skip if he had never returned my love in any way, for I am human, but God's love transcends even the purest form of motherly love.

With that new kind of love for my child came a tremendous sense of responsibility for his well-being. A new sense of urgency overwhelmed me as I realized my responsibility for what he became as a person and where he would spend eternity. For good or for ill, my influence on him might be greater than that of any other person in his life.

Skip would be affected not only by what I said and did, but to a greater extent by what I was. If my relationship with Jesus Christ was genuine, he would detect it. Conversely, a phony faith would not fool him at all. The responsibility frightened me. Human wisdom and ingenuity would not suffice. Even with the assistance of my godly husband, who was equally concerned about Skip's future, that would not be enough. We needed God's help.

"Dear Lord," I prayed, "the raising of this child is going to be too difficult for us to do alone. We simply don't know how. We want him to find the niche in life You have carved out for him. We want him to go to heaven when he dies. Those are our goals for him.

"But, Lord, You know his future already. If Skip is destined to become a rebel who will break our hearts and Yours too, then please take him while he is still a baby, before he is old enough to rebel. If You are going to let him live out his lifetime, let him live for You.

"Give us wisdom and patience to raise him as we should. We can't do it alone. Thank You, Lord."

Though I wept at the possibility, however remote, that Skip really might be taken, my prayer came straight from my heart. My love for him was so great that I preferred death for him rather than a rebellious life and an eternity apart from God.

As each new baby came, five in all, I prayed the same prayer for them. But God did not take any of them. We had the pleasure of nurturing each child to adulthood.

Those nurturing years involved adjustments of many kinds. Physically exhausting days came when all five children lived at home and took part in a variety of activities: church functions, Scouts, paper routes, piano lessons, hockey practice, and part-time jobs. Each whirled off in a different direction, and at times it seemed as though I whirled too. During one period, we had seven to chauffeur with one car; later we had seven chauffeurs and one car.

More than once during those busy days I seriously considered running away from it all. The only problem was that I didn't know where to run. Several possible destinations came to mind: Mother's home, a sister's farm, a hotel in California, or, best of all, a hut in Tahiti. After examining each possibility, however, none quite fit my needs.

I was trapped. Simply no place existed in the whole world to which one could run—until I discovered the sole avenue of escape that was available to me. I could run to God.

"The righteous cry and the LORD hears, and delivers them out of all their troubles" (Psalm

34:17). That was just what I needed; someone to listen to me. And God promised something my mom or sister could not give me; He would deliver me out of my trouble.

Falling to my knees, I told God all about my frustrations, my fatigue, my failures, my inadequacies. Remaining on my knees, in tears, until the burden of my problems had been lifted, I found the best escape route available.

In retrospect, it seems strange that I searched out every other possibility for escape from my problems before I turned them over to God. Yet I did that on many occasions. Finally, I did learn the lesson and ran to God first, but it took many years to come to that place.

In her book *Mama Doesn't Live Here Anymore,* Judy Sullivan tells how she actually did run away from her family. Leaving her husband and eleven-year-old daughter, she went to New York to seek a career. "I owe more to myself now than I do to you or my daughter," she explained to her husband. He finally divorced her.

Many times during the taxing days when all of the children were home, the same questions came to me. *How much do I owe my family? How much must I give? How much do I owe myself?* No easy answers could be found to those queries until I asked God for His view.

How much did God give?

If my love for my children was a miniature of God's love, then my standard of selflessness must also be patterned after His selflessness. Though we can never attain His level of unselfish love, it is a goal toward which we must strive.

Just about the time Skip outgrew his childish behavior and became a man, he left home to attend college. We had him when he wasn't always a pleasure; we had to give him to the world when he was. That did not seem quite fair. The next year Craig left, and within a very few years all five had gone.

One year we had a child in grade school, one in junior high, one in senior high, one in college, and one in graduate school. Adjustments became the order of the day. Some of them involved reversals, and many continue to this day.

Today my children worry about my personal well-being just as I worried about theirs. They thrill at my accomplishments just as I thrill at theirs.

How pleased I was when our youngster found his first part-time job; now they are pleased that I found one.

How proud I was when someone said my daughter was beautiful, or my son handsome; now they are proud when someone says I am pretty.

How I worried that one of my climbers might fall from the big oak and hurt himself; now the children worry that I will fall, not from the oak, but simply to the ground.

How I boasted that my child walked or talked at a certain age; now they boast that I ski—at my age.

How pleased I was with every healthy pound of weight my children gained; now they are pleased with every pound I lose.

Life for me today often appears to be backtracking. My role is to sit in the balcony of life more as an observer than as a participant. But as I watch my five offspring from a distance, all born-again believers in Christ busy in their chosen professions, how I thank God.

Although the adjustments were many, varied, and often difficult, He gave us the ability to cope with them. Thank God, He honored me with a "Ma" degree; I thank Him too for the adjustments—major and minor—that caused me to grow up in Him.

A New Kind of Twin

2

A New Kind of Twin

We have twins at our house: brothers. Not so unusual, except that our twins were born ten years apart! Not ten minutes, but ten years.

Skip, our oldest son, and Kent, our youngest, easily meet the dictionary qualifications for twins—"Two persons or things closely related or closely resembling each other."

Those two are not only closely related, but they also look alike and have similar personalities.

God surely must have had a very good reason for giving us two children who were so much alike. It seemed He was saying, "OK, Mom, I'm giving you one more opportunity. You had such a dreadful time raising Skip, I'm giving you a chance to demonstrate what you've learned. It will help to assuage your conscience, you understand."

My conscience did need comforting, all right,
and needed it badly. A lot of mistakes had been
made in handling my firstborn son. Recalling my
stern disciplining of him, I could cry even yet.
How I wish it had not been that way. Our next
three children had taught me much, and now I
was given a "twin" to complete my learning.

Skip was the little tyke I had to learn to love,
then to adjust to, because he upset our tranquil
marriage. We had enjoyed four years of harmon-
ious routine before he was born. Suddenly we had
neither harmony nor routine, just bedlam.

"He was a little rascal," said one of my sisters,
recalling Skip as a child.

He was indeed a rascal, I agreed, but only
because I made him that way. Had I displayed the
maternal qualities that should have characterized
my life; had I the knowledge, the godly wisdom
that should have been mine, he would not have
been such a rascal.

Skip, whose real name is Spencer, became a fine
Christian teenager and later a medical doctor. But
I take no credit for his accomplishments. Despite
my many blunders God stepped in and did for
him what was necessary in his life. God knew my
motive was right, and He rewarded me for that.
My methods, however, were far from right.

One of the problems I had while raising Skip
had to do with my background. For seven years
before his birth I had taught elementary school.
During those years I saw enough naughty, undis-

ciplined children to convince me that I would not have one like that. My kids were going to be obedient—obedient or else!

It was the *or elses* that gave me the problems, and those same *or elses* challenged Skip. He loved them! Our days seemed filled from morning to night with one challenge after another.

"Don't do that, Skip, or—" That was just the invitation my son needed to defy me. Without fail, he would do exactly what he had been asked not to do. Then, with a mischievous twinkle in his eyes and a grin on his face, he waited for my reaction.

I realize now I should not have challenged him in that way, but I didn't know it then. In a sense, I was promoting his defiance. As a result, "No, no, no!" to him meant just the opposite: "Yes, yes, yes!"

One incident in particular proved how determined Skip was and how equally determined—and ignorant—I was. He must have been about two, able to travel from one place to another quickly. As he played in the living room on the floor, he held a nail in his hand. We were building our home at the time, so it was not difficult to find nails lying about even though we tried to be careful.

Since nails belong in holes, Skip had found a suitable place for the one in his hand—an electrical outlet near the floor. Frightened, I said my "No, no's," took the nail from him, and returned to my work.

In a short time he found another object and was desperately trying to force it into the same outlet. I repeated my "No, no's," slapped his hands, took the object, and returned to my work.

In minutes, he was trying hard to poke something else into the outlet. After giving him a sharp reprimand, I spanked him. He whimpered ever so slightly, then found something else to poke.

After paddling him harder and moving him far from the area, I gave him something else to play with and then watched to see what he would do. He went back and poked again. How many times I spanked him that day is hard to remember, but it was far too many.

In despair, I finally plunked him in his crib. No outlets could be found there. He was safe, and I had a few minutes of peace—unsettled peace, to be sure, for I was troubled. That kind of disciplinary treatment came from a mother who truly loved her son.

Other skirmishes posed different problems, but the battle strategy remained identical: his will against mine. Being bigger, I always won. Our family physician heard me whimper one day, "I don't know what on earth to do with him, Doctor. He's so stubborn."

In his reassuring manner, the doctor said, "Be glad he's stubborn." His unusual reasoning didn't evoke any strange calm in me. That doctor did not have to live with Skip.

Life with our first child was not a very pleasant

experience. One day-long skirmish followed another, and the end result made neither of us happy. The older he grew, the more inventive he became, and the more frustrating my problems became. The time arrived when I could no longer put him in his crib for respite; I had to contend with him all day.

Had my husband been home during the day to help, it would have eased the burden. Skip was hardly awake when Walt left for work, and he didn't return much before the child's bedtime. The training of our son was clearly my responsibility, a burden almost too much to bear.

My guide for the training of my child came from Proverbs 23:13-14: "Don't fail to correct your children; discipline won't hurt them! They won't die if you use a stick on them! Punishment will keep them out of hell" (TLB).*

That was my first priority: to keep my children out of hell. To make them worthwhile, productive members of society whose primary interest was keeping other people out of hell was my second priority. Focusing on that one verse, I determined that strict discipline was the complete answer. But I was wrong. The Bible speaks of other kinds of training too. Punishment is only one form.

"Let love be your greatest aim" (1 Corinthians 14:1). To discipline with love was something I

The Living Bible.

knew nothing about. "The best kind of discipline is that which hurts the least," declared John C. Wynn in his book *How Christian Parents Face Family Problems*. My tool in discipline had been the kind that hurts the most.

Fortunately for Kent—and for me, too—by the time he came along God had taught me how to use love as a tool in his training. Because of my frustration with Skip, many hours had been spent on my knees in desperation. God had answered those pleas by teaching me a new concept. With a brand new life in my arms, I would need His help.

Before Kent's birth, we had had four babies—Skip, Craig, Curt, and Janet, our only girl. Craig, a chubby, good-natured child, changed our life-style very little. He was different from Skip because I was different. Sixteen months of training made me more relaxed with him than with my firstborn.

Curt was a blond, curly-haired bundle of goodness who seldom even cried. Janet, whom the boys called Princess, received the attention of a budding monarch as our only female. Then came Kent.

He was so much like Skip that we were amazed. He resembled him both in appearance and in personality. Neither baby sucked his thumb, although the other three did. Both required a lot of my attention, and both were inventive.

Fortunately for Kent, when he began to poke nails into outlets to gain my attention, I knew how to handle the problem a little better. His apparent defiance of my instructions did not constitute obstinacy or meanness. It was his method of attracting notice; he wanted his mother.

If after one reprimanding session, Kent returned to the same activity, I knew what to do. Stopping whatever else I was doing and picking him up from the floor, I cuddled him while rocking in the old-fashioned rocker. At first, his muscles seemed taut, rigid, and unyielding, but as I stroked, talked, and sang to him, those muscles relaxed.

In a few minutes, he was smiling. I continued to caress him until our friendship was firmly established again, until he felt loved. Then I placed him back on the floor with his toys where he played happily.

Our friendship continued for the rest of the day, often for two or more days. But when another display of defiance occurred, it was time for another session of loving attention. I cuddled him until those muscles of rebellion relaxed and we were friends again.

Kent rarely needed a spanking. He had a unique method of gaining my attention. At age three, he came to me one day and asked, "Mommy, what can I do for you?"

Do for me? Now that was a switch, for most three-year-olds are not interested in doing anything for anybody. I knew that Kent was mature for his age (ahem!), but I did not really think he was that mature.

My mother heart swelled with pride. Caressing

his upturned face and gazing into his eyes with new awareness, I tried to think of something he could do. Certainly I did not want to discourage his first grown-up request.

Picking up a book that had been left lying on a table, and glowing with pride, I said, "You're Mommy's big helper, aren't you? Why don't you put this book in the bookcase for me?"

Instead of being pleased, as I was certain he would, Kent merely puckered his mouth into a pout. "No, I don't wanna do that," he whined.

Before I could respond, he posed the question again, "What can I do for you, Mommy?"

His voice had the same pleading tone, and in order not to thwart my little darling I handed him one of his toys and said, "Put this in the toy box for me."

"I don't wanna do that. What can I do for you?"

Now I really was puzzled. "What do you want to do for Mother?" I asked. He must have had some specific job in mind.

Instead of answering my query, he merely asked the question again. But none of my suggestions pleased him. He simply didn't "wanna" do any of them. By that time, my patience tottered more than a little. Without solving the problem, I suggested he go outside to play with his sister.

Hardly a day passed that he didn't come to me at least once with the same request. Still, I could not determine what he really wanted. It seemed certain he wasn't looking for work.

One day a glimmer of wisdom came to me. When Kent came with the question, I picked him up from the floor, searched his blue eyes, and asked him, "What do you want Mommy to do for you?"

His reply came quickly. "Rockabye me in the rocking chair."

"Whew!" I sighed with relief. He had not wanted to do anything for me at all; he wanted me to do something for him. He wanted loving attention. Away went my proud thoughts about his superior mental growth. He was not really so unique after all.

He often asked the same question, but when he did I knew he simply wanted attention. Perhaps a drink of water, a cookie, or a change of clothing, but more often he just wanted me—and a little bit of loving in the old rocker.

Skip's apparent naughtiness was his way of getting my attention. He probably needed some loving rockabying too, but I was too insensitive to realize it. His taut little muscles were not caressed into compliance; they were spanked. My failures in that area still hurt, but God has forgiven me.

Kent today recalls one time when his discipline did not come in love taps. On his eighth birthday, he and a neighbor friend started a roaring fire in the dry grass. Another neighbor stamped out the blaze before it went out of control. Kent was soundly spanked, as reasoning alone would not have been a wise handling of the situation.

On the other hand, Skip did not receive *only* spankings. We loved him dearly, too. But he didn't receive the proper balance of correction. The Bible teaches that proper discipline is a combination of love and punishment. To find the correct balance requires wisdom that only God can give.

The training of my children is my job. The church cannot do that for me, nor can society, the community, or the schools. My goals must be clear-cut. For us it was twofold: we wanted each to know Jesus Christ in a personal way, and we wanted them to be influential in bettering our world by helping others as well to trust Christ.

Discipline is one of the necessary tools in order for us to realize those goals. Adjusting to our "twins" taught us valuable lessons in pursuit of our goals.

Two Kinds of Love

3

Two Kinds of Love

Before Walt and I married, we were certain ours would be the perfect union. So perfect, in fact, that anger, sullen silences, fights, and lack of consideration would be unthinkable.

After all, our six-year courtship had been like a peaceful cruise on a shimmering lagoon. Surely our wedded state would be an extension of that trouble-free voyage.

Walt and I met for the first time when Marge and I, college friends, spent two weeks in his church. We had come to teach summer Bible school, and Walt was the Sunday school superintendent. On our last day there, he asked to take me home.

Although I realized he was a very nice person, I was not at all romantically interested in him. He wrote to me after I returned home and I answered, but I saw him only once during the entire year.

The next spring, Walt wrote to tell me he was coming to see me—so he could meet my family. I was furious. "Who does he think he is, anyway?" I sputtered. "Coming without an invitation, at that!" Though tempted to tell him not to come, I decided that that probably would not be kind.

When the day arrived and he drove up in his big new Buick, my family was impressed. And when an immaculately dressed young man presented himself at the door, everyone beamed. Everyone, that is, except me. I was still furious.

My family loved him immediately and told me in private that I had to be crazy to be uninterested. Though fuming inside, I was polite to him. After all, he had driven several hundred miles to see me. Christian duty dictated that I should not be rude.

Actually, in retrospect I don't know why I didn't enjoy Walt more. A dedicated Christian, he was intelligent, neat, and clean. He had a good job, and he was single. What more could I want?

That evening he took me to one of our best restaurants for dinner. He was so gentlemanly, so handsome, so thoughtful, and so kind that I had to feel more than a little pride in him. Classmates and friends we encountered that evening showed obvious admiration as they met him.

Our conversation during dinner was both serious and jovial as we touched on a variety of subjects. My appreciation of Walt grew, and before the evening was over I realized what a fine young man he really was.

That night before leaving the car, he kissed me for the first time. *Wow!* As I went into the house, my heart throbbed with the thrill of it all. Sleep was a long time in coming that night, for I was too excited to relax.

Six years after our initial meeting in his church, we were married in my church. But during those six years we discussed a full range of subjects and participated in a wide variety of activities. I enjoyed his company and he enjoyed mine. We were truly in love.

After our wedding we spent one week in a secluded cabin on an island in Lake Vermillion, a perfect honeymoon retreat. That idyllic week was not the end of our honeymoon, however. It continued for almost four years. During that lengthy period, our marriage was just the way we knew it was going to be—trouble-free.

But then came our first battle. It triggered battle number 2 and battle number 3, until we discovered that we were just like the couples we knew we weren't going to be like.

My pregnancy was the initial spark that triggered the change. Up to that point, I had been teaching; a baby on the way meant I had to quit. That, in turn, meant our income was cut almost in half. While our income decreased, our expenses grew—skyrocketed would be a more apt term. Not only were we furnishing a nursery; we were also building our home.

Our checkbook became our first battleground.

As with many couples, we were opposite kinds of spenders. In our family, I'm the chintzy one; Walt was the liberal. The more generous he became, the more frightened I became and consequently the more chintzy (or *careful*, as I prefer to call it).

For that first almost four years, we had both enjoyed Walt's generous spending and lavish giving. We made a lot of friends and made many people happy. We could give generously because we had two incomes and few expenses, along with a modest bank account.

With an expanding family and larger living quarters, however, our excess quickly disappeared so that we had to change our spending pattern if we were to stay afloat.

That change was not made easily. In fact, the change was never made. For Walt to change would have meant a complete altering of personality. He was generous and gregarious, ingrained facets of his personality.

So I was given the task of trying to balance our income with our expenses. What a task that was! Walt continued to spend, while I continued to agonize over bills. Although concerned about our checkbook balance, he wrote checks as if he had no concern at all. Only once did he ever attempt to balance our checkbook, and that was a disaster.

Thirty years of sensible chats and senseless spats did not change our financial manipulations in the least. Battle number 1 was never won, but at least we agreed to disagree.

Battle number 2 also resulted from our differing personalities. Walt was sociable; I was shy. For months after we were married, we were satisfied to be alone. We had many casual friends, but no involved relationships. I liked it that way. Soon it became apparent that Walt did not.

Having grown up in a large, rather boisterous family and a happy, active church, he loved the interchange in both. I grew up on a rather isolated farm and had little contact with church.

Walt loved people by the dozen; I liked them in ones or twos. Walt loved to entertain crowds; I loved isolated corners. He wanted me to entertain many people. That very thought frightened me; I preferred tea for two.

We compromised by entertaining small groups on special occasions, but that was not his preference. Battle number 2 was never really won by either, but again we learned how to disagree while remaining agreeable.

Battle number 3 still involved a skirmish of traits. Happiness for me meant organization and planning; for Walt happiness meant spontaneity. What chaos resulted when my staid plans collided with his spur-of-the-moment decisions. Though that battle was never won either, we both learned important lessons.

The rest of our battles will not be recorded, for most of them, like the others, had no winner. At one point, they became so frequent and so devastating that the word *divorce* actually crept into our verbal fight.

What had happened to our "perfect" marriage? What had gone wrong? More important, what was the solution?

Although we didn't realize it at the time, we learned later that the problems we faced were similar to those that plague every marriage. No two can exist in the closeness of marriage bonds without some friction. In every close alliance, problems may have a different twist, but the basic precept remains the same.

If marriage automatically means problems, our job was to find a solution—one that would not only keep us married to each other, but also would bring us real happiness as well. We discovered our marriage needed a different kind of love.

I married Walt because he met my qualifications. He was a Christian; he was kind, generous, intelligent, friendly, and loving.

Walt married me because I met his qualifications. I was a Christian; I was quiet, shy, had a job, and who knows what other reasons he might have had.

He married me because he loved and admired me; I married him because I loved and admired him.

Each of us married *because* . . . That was the first kind of love we experienced—*because love*.

After our honeymoon, we discovered traits in one another that disturbed us. Icebergs in our sea of matrimony began to surface, chilling our voyage. Not only that, but we realized that colliding with any one of them could have wrecked our precious craft and destroyed our cargo. A collision such as that must be avoided.

In answer to prayer, we learned how to change our course. We discovered that marriage needed another kind of love—*in-spite-of love*. That kind of love is unselfish.

Because love is selfish. It says: he is handsome, therefore he makes me feel proud; he is kind, therefore he will comfort me; he is reliable, therefore he will give me security.

In-spite-of love is different. It says: he is careless, therefore, even though it will make more work for me, I will try to compensate for his weakness and patiently endure; he is moody, and that disturbs my peace of mind, but I will do my best to help him cultivate a better mood; he is a spendthrift, and that makes me feel insecure, but I will try to understand his generous spirit and charitable nature.

How can one continue to love a mate whose glaring imperfections destroy any sense of security and peace of mind? *In-spite-of love*—is it really possible at all? If it is, then how is it cultivated?

Only with the help of God can such a selfless love become a reality. After all, He originated marriage in the first place, and He alone can make it successful. "In everything you do, put God first, and he will direct you and crown your efforts with success" (Proverbs 3:6, TLB).

If we really wanted our marriage to be a success, and surely we did, we knew we needed divine help. *In-spite-of love* is God's brand. He loves me in spite of what I am or what I do. He loves everyone, though He hates our sin. At our request, He can teach us how to experience His kind of love.

The first prerequisite is to want to love another in that way. We certainly wanted to, not just for the joy and satisfaction Walt and I would realize, but also for the continued security and happiness our children would enjoy. The collapse of our marriage could destroy all of us. Neither of us wanted that.

Second, we had to acknowledge our inability to create that kind of love ourselves. It had to come from God. We spent much time searching the Scriptures and praying together. But the answer did not come in one great flash. Gradually we began to discover that the imperfections and differences were not so intolerable.

With that discovery, our love for each other blossomed, transcending undesirable and irritating traits. The personality differences remained, but they were not so irksome anymore. How God accomplished that feat is still a mystery to me.

Eventually our marriage matured until it was on a far better basis than when we first married. *Because love* prompted our marriage; *in-spite-of love* held it intact. The adjustments that took place as we learned how to love God's way were certainly not easy, but they were beneficial. God made the changes possible.

Ain't Got No Money

4

Ain't Got No Money

One evening a friend heard a conversation between Kent, then five, and his young friend Martha.

"My Mom and Dad are really poor. They ain't got no money at all." Kent spoke in a solemn tone of voice while busily servicing his toy cars.

"Really?" Martha asked sympathetically.

"Yup. They ain't got no money." Kent's face brightened and he smiled as he continued triumphantly, "They got lotsa checks."

Our son's evaluation of our financial situation was really quite correct, even though he lacked understanding about a number of concepts—including our use of checks. Compared with the income of many American families, we probably would have been considered anything but wealthy.

On the economic scale, we stood on the sagging

side of average. Somehow that image had been
conveyed to Kent, even though we seldom discussed money problems within the hearing of our
children. Had Kent known how often our checks
quivered on the verge of bouncing, he would not
have ended his conversation so triumphantly.

One of America's humorists remarked, "I've been
rich, and I've been poor, and if I could choose, I'd
be rich." Having never been rich, I cannot argue
with the man on the basis of experience. But this I
do know: being "not rich" also has its rewards.

That statement should be qualified, however. A
lack of necessary funds is tragic when the one in
need also lacks a personal, working relationship
with our rich God. Then he is very poor indeed.

On the other hand, if one has become a child of
God through faith in Jesus Christ, that relationship opens the way to God's riches. As God's
children, we are His heirs and have access to His
bounteous possessions.

We decided to take at face value the promise in
Philippians 4:19 (TLB), "And it is he who will
supply all your needs from his riches in glory,
because of what Christ Jesus has done for us."
From experience, we learned that God keeps His
promises.

As a result, we had everything needed for the
family, plus many things we could have lived
without. Life was an exciting experience as we
learned firsthand some of the unique methods
God used to supply our necessities.

Two decisions early in our marriage determined to a great extent our financial future. The first was our decision to have children, all five of them, and the second decision was for me to discontinue teaching when our first child arrived.

When I became a full-time mother and home-maker, ours would be a one salary home. Both of the decisions were made willfully, and we regret-ted neither one of them, even though the choice did mean that we could never hope to become affluent.

Our New Year's resolutions reminded me of Mark Twain's wry comment: "This year I shall live within my income, even if I must borrow the money to do it." Our financial escapades, exciting though they were, may have appeared foolhardy to the unbeliever.

We found that one and one are not necessarily two. The sum of those two numbers plus God might equal anything. But who would believe such foolish mathematics if he hadn't experienced it?

The first lesson we had to learn—the hard way, by experience—was that we had to meet certain requirements to draw on God's bank account. "If you do this," God says, "then I will do that." "No good thing does He withhold from those who walk uprightly" (Psalm 84:11). "If you keep My com-mandments, you will abide in My love" (John 15:10).

Then there is the awful alternative. "If . . . you

do not obey Me, but act with hostility against Me, then I will act with wrathful hostility against you" (Leviticus 26:27-28).

One "if then" command we had to learn—and learn again each week when our paycheck came—is found in Malachi 3:10 where God promises that if we bring our tithes He will pour out such blessings that we won't have room to receive them.

If we give God a tithe, or one tenth of the paycheck, He will pour out blessings upon us. With a promise like that, it would seem we should not have a problem obeying it, but we did.

It does seem strange and inconsistent to say to God, "I'd rather keep Your tenth of my paycheck than receive Your blessing." But we did say that, in effect, more than once. After many, many paychecks, we finally learned that His blessings far exceeded the value of a tithe.

Part of our battle with that scriptural directive stemmed from the fact that it is not a logical conclusion from a purely human standpoint. What teacher of mathematics has ever taught that one can buy as much with 90 percent as he can with 100 percent?

We learned that 90 percent plus God always equals 100 percent—often more. It meant trusting in God, whom we could not see, instead of trusting in the money that we could see and actually hold in our hands. That required faith.

While we parents were learning the value of faith as we tithed, we taught our children its value, too. Craig's experience as a teenager was typical of the kind of adventure we all enjoyed with our money.

Craig wanted to become an electrical engineer with a major in computers. Having completed one year in our local college, he was contemplating a transfer to the University of Minnesota to complete the course. Since each of our children must assume his own college expenses, Craig worked during the summer at a paper mill. He saved every penny he could so he would have enough for the year's tuition, room, and board.

Late in August, he calculated his earnings and learned that he had saved enough money to pay his tuition and almost enough for his room and board. But he had nothing for books, clothing, and incidentals that would certainly be needed. Nor had he paid his tithe for several weeks.

Craig decided he "owed the Lord" about $85. That presented a problem, for his working days during the summer had nearly ended, and he knew he would never earn all he needed. The battle raged in his mind.

Eventually, without any parental advice, Craig resolved the matter by sending his entire tithe to an evangelistic organization. Two weeks later he received a letter informing him that he had been granted a scholarship of $850, ten times the amount he had given to the Lord's work. What indescribable joy we all experienced as we witnessed anew the faithfulness of God.

Craig found his needs supplied each year, graduated, and is presently in his chosen occupation. Though God does not always promise a tenfold return, He does promise to meet our needs and shower us with good. The nonmonetary blessings often are priceless. We consider our family's health to be one of those invaluable blessings.

God's methods in providing us with necessities often bordered on the miraculous. Often we recalled the children of Israel and their wanderings in the desert. "And I have led you forty years in the wilderness; your clothes have not worn out on you, and your sandal has not worn out on your foot" (Deuteronomy 29:5).

God helped us with our clothing needs as well. Our two oldest boys, Skip and Craig, just a year apart, usually had their clothing bought at the same time. When both were in junior high, we bought each of them three pairs of trousers that we hoped would last through the school year.

Those two active, growing teenagers wore their three pairs of trousers to school not just for one year but for two full years. At the end of the second year, their trousers still looked almost new, with no patches. And even more amazing, the boys had not outgrown them. They could easily have worn them another year.

Though the boys were not completely happy to wear the same pants for so long, they did not protest too vigorously. That was not a forty-year span like the Israelites had, but it seemed quite a feat to the mother of growing boys.

As you can imagine, shopping for clothing for our seven members proved to be an expensive item in our budget. To cope with the high costs, we usually did our buying in the off-season. Before embarking on each shopping trip, we prayed that we would find exactly the items needed at an affordable price. Watching God answer those prayers made our shopping trips exciting for all of us.

In addition to clothing, housing costs also posed a problem. Take the plumbing incident, for example.

Something apparently had lodged in one of our underground sewer pipes, completely clogging every drain in the house. In a large house, such a problem becomes more than an unpleasant inconvenience—more like a mild catastrophe. We tried everything we knew to dislodge whatever culprit was causing the problem.

Although we hoped to avoid a plumber's bill, it seemed we had exhausted every possibility. Suddenly we remembered prayer. "Dear Lord," I prayed, "You can see the mess we have. You know, too, that we've done everything we can to correct the problem. Now, Father, since You are omnipotent and can do anything You want to do, please unplug the sewer for us."

We watched the drain to see what would happen. The stagnant pool stood still. We waited. Then we thought we detected a tiny movement. We waited some more. Yes, it really was moving. Suddenly there was a gurgle, a swirl, and the sewage slurped back into the pipes where it belonged. What a relief! Much more important, we were reminded again that God was interested in our plight.

Another adventure requiring divine intervention involved our purchase of cars. We always delayed our buying until we could no longer drive our car safely. The delay stemmed from the fact that we could never quite stretch our money to include a car payment.

My husband believed that buying a used car was "buying someone else's troubles," so we always bought new cars. Then came the adventure of paying monthly for our purchase. We never knew where the funds came from, as our income did not increase, but we never missed a monthly payment. Even more astounding to us was the fact that we seemed to have as much money left over for living as we did before we bought the car, another of God's beautiful miracles.

When driving tired old cars, which they all eventually became, we always trusted God to get us to our destination. When we drove brand new cars, somehow we trusted the car to get us there. In retrospect, I wonder how wise it was for us to shift our faith from faith in God to faith in a new car. But wise or not, that is what we did.

Teaching our children honesty in the handling of money had high priority in our training. As a result, "There's money in the cup" was heard often in our household. In a corner shelf in our kitchen stands a planter in the shape of a bunny in which there is cash. Just why we called it a "cup" instead of a bunny, we'll never know—except that it is easier to say.

At any rate, whenever one of the kids needed change for lunch, school supplies, or grocery items I would say, "There's money in the cup." Each child had the freedom to take from the container as much money as he needed. If he took more than he needed, it was his responsibility to return the unused portion.

Not once did we parents or any other member of the family question a child as to how much he took from the cup. No one ever questioned another's honesty. Although the cash was always accessible to everyone, I feel certain that no one ever "stole" a cent from the cup. We all expected everyone else to be completely honest, and as a result everyone was honest.

The reverse might well have been true. If we had been suspicious of each other and questioned the honesty of others, they may have set out to prove to us that they were, indeed, exactly as we suspected they were. If a child believes he is not trusted, often he becomes untrustworthy.

That principle holds true in other facets of raising children as well. A child will be just about the way a parent expects him to be.

Contrary to popular custom, our children never received an allowance. They learned the principles of economics—spending, saving, and tithing—from the use of their own earnings.

Each of the boys assumed the responsibility of a paper route as soon as he was old enough and wise enough to convince a manager he was capable. All four continued as newsboys until they were sixteen.

While still in high school, each child had a part-time job. Craig and Skip delivered clothing for a dry cleaning establishment, and Kent worked as an orderly in a nursing home. Janet earned her money by babysitting until she became a "car-hop" for a drive-in restaurant.

Home responsibilities—mowing the lawn, shoveling snow—were assumed by each one without pay. Those jobs represented their contribution for the privilege of being a part of the family. That felt right to us; it may not be right for someone else.

Some of our children are conservative spenders, while others are more liberal. Whether their money habits would have been different under other tutelage, we will never know. We were successful in raising five honest tithers, one of our goals.

Though big and comfortable, our home is not elegant. Though we live on a lake, we have never owned a large boat. Though trails abound, we have never owned a snowmobile. Though the lawn is huge, we have never owned a riding mower. Though we have had many drivers, we have shared one car.

For some reason, our children never clamored for such conveniences, even though most of our neighbors had them. Sometimes I wonder why they did not. Our financial adjustments, one of our mightiest hurdles, also proved one of the most rewarding adjustments in our marriage. And the fact that "we ain't got no money," as Kent put it, has taught us spiritual lessons we would not have learned otherwise.

The Mood of the House

5

The Mood of the House

It was the poet Edgar Guest who wrote, "It takes a heap o' living to make a house a home."

Those of us privileged to live and grow up in warm, loving homes know well the wisdom of his words. Good living did make them homey places.

Not just any kind of living makes houses into homes—it must be a certain kind, a special kind. It takes a heap of happy living to make houses into homes. Unhappy living never quite does the job.

Unhappy living creates an atmosphere, a mood that is not at all homelike. In fact, it tends to make people uncomfortable, for it repels rather than attracts.

The people of China have a name for the mood of a house. They call it *fung-shui*. When people live together harmoniously, they say the *fung-shui* is good. When the occupants fight and curse, the *fung-shui* is bad. Although we in America have no name for the mood of a house, it is there nevertheless. Sensitive people can feel that mood.

Walt and I went to the home of new friends one day to help them move into their new home. Much cleaning, unpacking, and arranging had to be done to get them settled. Though we had no idea what went on in that home before we arrived, the place seemed charged with electric sparks—what teens today call bad vibes.

The couple acted pleasantly toward us and expressed thanks for our assistance, but fireworks must have taken place before we arrived. The mood, the atmosphere of that house, became so distressing that I could not stand it. My husband took me home, though we gave no real reason for leaving.

Other homes have had unpleasant atmospheres in which we felt unwelcome, but never before had we been in one so filled with static. The homes of the majority of my friends are warm, friendly, and comfortable.

How do parents forge homes out of mere houses? What elements combine to make the place a refuge from the hostility of the world?

First of all, there must be love—love that envelops the entire family. When genuine love exists between parents, that affection usually spills over so that children are loving, too. Conversely, when parents argue and fight, children are likely to do the same.

Second, our home should be a means to an end, not an end in itself.

Mrs. M., extremely proud of her new, well-furnished house and equally proud of her reputation as a housekeeper, had four children. Every morning, promptly at eight, she sent her children outside, regardless of weather conditions. After locking the doors, she polished and scrubbed and cleaned until the house was spotless.

If a child came to the door crying she would ask, "Are you bleeding?" If the answer was yes, she bandaged the wound and quickly shoved the child outside again. At noon, they came in for lunch, went to bed for naps, then spent the rest of the day outdoors.

Everyone in the neighborhood observed the strange behavior. That mother's house was more important to her than her children. She was not unlike the man, a furniture store owner, who said, "If I ever catch one of my kids with his foot on the furniture, I'll knock his block off."

That man and Mrs. M. both have a wrong focus. My children were more important to me than either my house or my furnishings. My primary purpose in owning both—to make life more comfortable for my family—included the freedom to curl up on the sofa when one desired. We did not condone malicious destruction; neither did we insist on a house so hallowed that our kids couldn't relax in it.

Our living room had that lived-in look—sofa pillows askew and books in leap-frog position on every table. We liked it that way; so did our kids. Ours was a *living* room—not a display room.

Emotions of family members help make up the atmosphere of the home. Every person affects that mood to some extent, but the mother wields the greatest influence. Each mother should evaluate her own abilities and weaknesses and try to work within those guidelines.

Mothers who can involve themselves in a variety of organizations and still do a good job of mothering are to be admired, but I am not one of them. Tenseness characterizes my attitude when I attempt too much. And when I become tense, the entire family suffers. So I limited my activities to those I considered most valuable.

At the outset, church became my first priority. Even then, conflicts sometimes arose between the needs of my family and those of the church. In the face of those conflicts, I had to choose—and that often proved difficult.

My overriding desire to serve God initially convinced me that church functions should come first, even though my family needed me too. But I seldom had peace of mind about decisions like that.

Finally, after I prayed about the conflicts, God gave me new insights into my dual role as mother and churchworker. He taught me clearly that my first responsibility must be family. No one else could do my job at home.

If I failed to teach the children, they would not

be taught. If I failed to discipline them properly, they would not be disciplined. If I failed to guide them, they would not be guided. If I failed to love them, they would not be loved. Others could do my job in the church, but no one else could do my job with my own children. They had to be my private mission.

What a relief it was to realize that nurturing my family was serving God at the same time. That did not mean I was inactive in the church. For twenty years I taught a high school Sunday school class and served in other ways as well. But the conflict between church and family no longer existed. Both had their place, but family was my personal responsibility.

Walt served as Sunday school superintendent for thirty-five years. He also served in many other church activities, but we never forgot that raising our children in a Christlike manner remained top priority. When we became so involved—in church or elsewhere—that we were grouchy and tired at home, we knew we had to curtail our activities somewhere. Grouches do not reflect Christ.

Vance Havner wrote, "The Lord told His disciples to 'come ye apart and rest awhile.' What He meant was, 'Come ye apart and rest awhile, or come ye apart.'" Some people need more than others, but all of us need rest in order that we will not come apart at the seams.

To keep from falling apart, I took a short nap every afternoon. For me, that was essential. Our

day began at 4:30 A.M. After a nutritious breakfast, I tackled my day's work with vengeance. By
noon, I was tired. At times, I would continue working all afternoon, but that made me too tired.

When the children came home from school, I
was cross. Instead of listening with interest to the
tales they had bottled up within them, I was too
tired to care. A nap changed that.

I am a morning person; the nap proved to be
just what I needed. It gave me the equivalent of
two mornings every day. It was what my children
needed too, for it made me a happier person.

"It takes me all morning to wake up," a friend
said to me one day. "If I were to nap, it would take
the rest of the afternoon to come alive." Since she
was at her best in the afternoon, for her to nap
would have been self-defeating.

Each of us is different; individually we must
decide how best to cope with life's demands. But
this much is certain: children need happy, rested,
interested, patient mothers if the atmosphere of
the home is to be pleasant. Each mother must
decide how she best can accomplish that task.

Recalling events in my own childhood, I remember that aromas played an important part in my
life—the smell of freshly baked bread or the pun-
gent waft of rhubarb boiling. Even now, I never
smell cinnamon but my mind flits back to a certain rainy day in my childhood.

My brother and I had sloshed home from school,
a two-and-a-half-mile hike, in the rain. By the time

we reached home, we were chilled; our clothes, dripping wet, clung to us. My dress bound my legs so that I stumbled when I ran. What a miserable sight we were!

Before we opened the kitchen door, a delicious aroma greeted us. Mom had been baking. On the kitchen table twelve fat loaves of bread and a pan of gooey cinnamon rolls awaited our arrival. We forgot our misery as we filled our stomachs with yummy, warm bites.

If a pleasure so simple as eating a warm cinnamon roll on a rainy day could make such a permanent impression upon my mind, I determined to fill my children's minds with equally pleasurable occasions. Each day I tried to have something baking, or just baked, when they arrived home from school. That was not always possible, but the likely prospect must have had something to do with their punctuality in coming home after school.

Skip recently recalled those early days. "I used to think how dumb it was to bake in the afternoon," he said, laughing. "I wondered why you didn't bake in the morning so you could hide the goodies. Then we couldn't have snitched so many."

Humor and good fun enhance the mood of any home. My husband deserved the credit for that dimension in our household. Not only was our home fun-filled; at times it appeared almost to rock with lighthearted activity. Walt's playfulness, pranks, laughter, and his unique, deliberately twisted vocabulary amused all of us. Chicken and dumplings, for example, he called "chicken and dumb things," because he didn't like them.

One Sunday, while vacationing in a cabin in a remote area of northern Minnesota, one of the children asked, "Dad, where are we going to church today?" We knew of no church within a radius of fifty miles.

Walt, whom all of us knew never touched alcohol, gazed at the tavern across the road. Then, with a mischievous twinkle in his eyes and a grin on his face he said, "Well, kids, I suppose we could go to the *tavern-acle!*"

A lighthearted father who enjoyed his children, Walt romped with them when they were little and camped, hunted, and fished with them when they were older. Humor and good sense punctuated every activity. He made life fun; we all loved him.

My place still lies in the family home. The children—now adults—call it the "rest home," because it is a place of relaxation for them. When they feel the need of an intermission from their busy vocations, they find it there. That makes me happy, because the same need for relaxation occasionally took me back to my childhood home too.

For me, the "rest home" was a simple farmhouse tucked in an isolated area of forest. The buildings have burned, the yard is in weeds, but I can still see in my mind the poppies, peonies, and bachelor buttons growing there.

The spruce, though scorched by fire, stand tall,

and a gnarled elm still has its place in the back-yard. Under that tree, we ate our meals on hot, summer days or swayed on the tire swing that hung from its branches.

From the moment I left the car, I relaxed. A carefree kid again, I ran. My tensions drained, and I felt so light I could almost have flown. Laughing as I ran from one familiar landmark to another in search of souvenirs, I almost smelled Mom's cinnamon rolls again. In no time at all, new strength surged through my veins.

Coping with my taxing world once again seemed possible. Memories of happiness and security enjoyed in that humble place refreshed me just as they did when I was a child. My present home offers the same kind of respite for my offspring; for that I'm grateful to God, who made it all possible.

Dr. Walter Menninger, psychiatrist, wrote: "Current estimates are that from 600,000 to one million adolescents run away from home annually; most are from white suburbs, at least half are girls, and many are no older than 13 or 14."

What a challenge to parents—that we might improve the mood, the atmosphere, in our homes!

A Joke on God

6

A Joke on God

It was 6:30 A.M. and time for our usual family devotions. My husband had had his breakfast and was ready for work, but our five children remained in their pajamas. Kent, our toddler, snuggled in my arms; Janet curled up in her daddy's arms, while the three older children drooped in over-stuffed chairs or relaxed in front of the warm air register in the living room. We had just twenty minutes before my husband had to leave for work.

In terms of bright-eyed concentration, that may not have been the ideal time, but it was the only time of day when we could be certain that every member of the family would be present and uninterrupted. Our devotions became a daily ritual.

With a ten-year age span between our youngest and oldest, we chose to read from a Bible story-book. Even our small kiddies not only maintained interest, but also seemed captivated by the fast-moving Bible stories related in their language. We read through the book so many times we wore it out and had to obtain a new binding.

One morning, I had finished reading a Bible story, Daddy, Skip, and Craig had prayed, and it was Curt's turn. He was five years old. He started in his usual serious manner, but then he said something that startled all of us. "And God, bless Mommy when she goes downtown to work today. Amen."

That isn't so funny, unless you realize that I did not work downtown. In fact, I didn't work outside the home at all. What prompted such a strange prayer? All eyes were fixed on Curt. "Why did you say that?" someone asked. "You know Mom doesn't work downtown."

A mischievous twinkle in his eyes, Curt tossed his curly blond head roguishly. "Ha, ha, ha," he laughed. "A joke on God."

For a moment, we were so stunned we were speechless. It was so out of character for Curt to say such a thing. He was a deep, thoughtful boy.

Finally, his father regained his sense of balance and kindly explained the futility of trying to fool God. "Son," Walt said, "God knows everything— absolutely everything. We can't fool Him or play jokes on Him, even though we would sometimes like to very much."

Walt reminded Curt of the truth of God's omniscience—a truth I suspect he knew already. If he had not known, he wouldn't have laughed so heartily at his own attempt at making jokes. Most of us still try to fool God in one way or another. We aren't very different from Curt.

Reliving the "joke on God" incident has brought a good many chuckles, but another family experience produced an emotion that was anything but amusing. It was, in fact, one of the most soul-piercing, disturbing experiences this mother has had.

It was a chilly October. Since our youngsters had a four-day weekend, we rented a rustic lake cabin for our last vacation fling of the year. In the living room was an old-fashioned woodburning stove, the only source of heat for the two-bedroom cottage. We chose the cabin for that very reason.

All of us enjoyed the smell and sound of crackling birch logs and the coziness of its variable heat. It provided an interesting change from the constant temperature of our home.

Before going to bed each night, my husband filled the stove with wood and closed all of the drafts. He wanted to maintain some measure of heat throughout the night and still conserve some hot coals for starting the fire in the morning.

At best, it was not easy to control. Usually, the cabin was too warm when we went to bed and too cool when we awoke in the morning. But that only added to the fun of cabin vacationing.

Although the rest of the family occupied the bedrooms, Craig chose to sleep on the couch in the living room. He was near the stove, so he felt the extremes of temperature more than the rest of the family did.

One night he had a horrible nightmare, perhaps triggered by the heat from the stove. His pitiful moaning awakened me.

"Oh, Mama," he said in a voice of desperation, "it's hot down here! Oh, Mama!"

After a moment's silence, I heard his triumphant declaration, "I'm getting out of here! Do you hear that, devil? I'm getting out of here!"

My own heart nearly burst with anguish. My son thought he was in hell. Rushing to his bedside to awaken him, to console him, I assured him it was only a dream. He finally slept again.

Though I returned to my bed, I was not able to sleep. For a few moments, I had experienced the sheer torment that a mother (or father) must feel when a child refuses redemption—refuses Christ's love. Craig had suffered a terrible nightmare. Over and over, his pitiful words tumbled about in my mind. *Thank God, it was not a reality but a dream from which we could all awaken.*

As I lay quietly, sleep eluding me, I prayed perhaps more fervently than I had ever prayed before in my life. First, I thanked God for the experience; it gave me a tiny glimpse of the agony of a lost soul. From now on, I would be more diligent in my concern not only for my own children, but for others as well.

Then I asked for a double portion of all the qualities needed to be a successful mother—wisdom, strength, patience, and even humor. My needs were more than I could ever supply alone. I needed God's help. Then I vowed to do everything I could to teach my kids to love God and obey Him as well.

"Kids learn by osmosis," wrote Dr. Christine Beasley in her book *Democracy in the Home*. If that is true, it is not enough that I do everything I ought to do; I must also be everything I ought to be. To be a successful doer, I must first of all be that kind of person. Being must precede doing.

"For good or ill," declared Dr. Beasley, "what we are drowns out anything we try to say." If that is true, then any attempt to deceive our children is almost as futile as playing jokes on God. We simply cannot get away with it.

If we want our children to love God, we must first love Him genuinely. If we want them to obey Bible principles, we must be obedient. A phony life and feigned faith transmit phoniness to our off-spring. If we want them to be genuine, we must be genuine too.

When Janet was about ten years of age, she fell and broke a front tooth—a central incisor. She came crying to me, her hands cupped over a bleeding mouth, and a beautiful permanent tooth dan-

Skip had the presence of mind to place the tooth back in its socket before we rushed her to the dentist. Shaking his head sadly, the dentist said, "I'm very sorry. I'm afraid the tooth is lost. Medical books don't offer much hope that a broken tooth like this will ever weld together and be strong enough to stand the pressure it receives. I'll wire it in place, anyway, just in case. Bring her back in two weeks."

For any girl to lose a front tooth is a tragedy of sorts. The psychological blow is far more traumatic for her than the expense of replacing the tooth. Boys somehow seem to manage better with capped or chipped teeth, as if to enhance their tough masculine image. But for a girl, it is something quite different.

As we returned home, our fears began to surface. Dare we pray for a miracle? Suppose we prayed and the tooth did not fuse and grow together. Would our children lose their faith in the supernatural ability of our omnipotent God? Could we take that chance?

But suppose we did pray and the tooth was saved. What a powerful lesson that would be! A miracle of that magnitude would bolster their faith so that they would never forget it.

We decided to ask for a miracle. We saw that miracle take place. Though happy with the result, our dentist shook his head in amazement. He could hardly believe that the tooth actually grew in place, even with X rays as proof. Now, more than ten years later, the tooth appears to be perfect. Janet's smile is our constant reminder that God is still a worker of miracles.

Craig remembers an experience in which God answered a weighty prayer for him. On a typical Minnesota winter evening, cold and crisp, his glasses became fogged as he delivered his evening papers. He took them off and put them in his jacket pocket. When he finished his route and arrived home, the glasses were gone. He had lost them.

The loss was a serious matter, for he needed them badly and had no extra pair. How does one locate an object so small and colorless in a snowdrift? His route covered more than a mile of snow-covered blocks. Besides that, it was now dark.

They must at least make an effort to find them, so Craig and his father set out on their "impossible" search. Before they left, they prayed that God would help them in their task.

Craig's route zigzagged from one back door to a front door, across lots, over fences, and past vicious dogs. Even in daylight, to retrace the route was not easy. In the dark, it was even more difficult. But they continued on, feeling a bit more dejected with each passing block.

Suddenly, with a spark of revelation, Craig remembered he had jumped from one back porch into an inviting snow bank. Just maybe, his glasses might have fallen out in that leap. But even if they had, could they ever be located in all the snow?

When they returned to the porch, they discovered the deep holes made by his feet as he leaped. With the light from a flashlight, they searched the area. Was that a reflection? Something shining in the snow? Sparkling snowflakes?

Almost covered with snow, the glasses suddenly appeared. They were exposed just enough to reflect a tiny ray of light—enough to be found. Two very happy people returned home. God had answered another family prayer request. Once again He had reinforced our faith in His omnipotent ability.

In our home is an old wooden puzzle that has been passed down to us from previous generations. The puzzle consists of eighteen oddly shaped pieces which, when placed together correctly, form a cube of sorts. It is a difficult puzzle to master— difficult, that is, until you discover the one particular piece that is the key.

Take out that one piece, the key, and the puzzle falls apart into a hopeless heap. So long as the key is in place, however, the puzzle cannot be taken apart no matter how one tries. It remains a unit.

That puzzle is somewhat like our family, which consists of seven distinct personalities, each unique and different. To fit us together as a unit, to place us under one roof to function in harmony would have been an absolute impossibility had it not been for one key piece.

That key is Jesus Christ. With the key in its

proper place, the center, our family is an entity. If we remove Him, we tumble into a hopeless mass of ill-fitting pieces without form or utility.

Jesus Christ is the key to unity and the source of love and wisdom. Without Him, we would have failed miserably. To be genuine and transparent before God—and before children as well—has been our goal.

Though we have blundered many times, we have sincerely tried to be honest—to play no devious jokes. We thank God for His clear direction along the way.

Those Tantalizing Teens

7

Those Tantalizing Teens

"Hey, Mom," reminded my oldest son, "it's my birthday tomorrow. Betcha forgot it. Will you make me a German sweet chocolate cake? Will you?"

Forget Skip's birthday? His thirteenth? No, I did not forget, but somehow I didn't share his enthusiasm. In fact, I had looked ahead to that fateful day with a paralyzing kind of fear. May nineteenth meant that I would have a teenager to contend with, and I was frightened. Teenagers always meant trouble, I thought, and I didn't want our peace-loving household to be disrupted in any way.

And if that was not enough to worry about, the following year—just sixteen months away, to be exact—Craig too would become a teen. The anticipation almost made me ill. How I wished that I had the ability to turn back time or cause it to stop indefinitely so that my kids would never have to join that dreadful teenage scourge.

My dread stemmed from information I had read about other parents and their adolescents. Many parents weep as they tell of the wild escapades in which their children became involved. Insurance companies consider their greatest risk a teenager behind the wheel of a car. To top it all, some psychologists say that a youth must rebel in order to develop in a normal way; it is his initiation into adulthood.

With all of that background material in mind, I assumed that our experiences with our family would not be any different from the majority of other families, since we were average. A sense of defeat convinced me that the only sensible alternative was to brace myself for the inevitable.

From teenhood forward, I should expect sullen disobedience, occasional visits from the police, car accidents, brawls, drug indulgence, drinking, premature marriages, and who knows what else. Now I would join the ranks of mothers who lay awake nights awaiting the arrival of a teen unconcerned about curfews. The future I envisioned was certainly not one eagerly awaited.

In retrospect, how very foolish a mother I was. How foolish to spend my days and nights worrying about the future and its problems instead of concentrating on the present. How foolish to fret about imaginary events that I was certain would come to pass, but in reality never did. What a waste of time. What a dissipation of energy. What a lack of faith. What sin.

D. L. Moody once said, "I have never met a man who has given me as much trouble as myself." No one has given me more trouble than myself—certainly not my teenagers.

Actually, the years during which they were easing their way into adulthood comprised the most enjoyable years we had in raising our family. Each year, it seemed, a closer bond of fellowship and understanding developed between us. When the children left home for college, they left an emptiness that was strangely filled with dozens of happy memories.

Why were we spared the heartache that so many parents experience? Why did our teens remain our friends during those difficult years of growing up? Why were there no dragons in our generation gap?

Would that I could tell you, that I could spell out in black and white the secret, so that every parent could enjoy his family as much as we have enjoyed ours. But I cannot. Personalities and circumstances vary too much for that.

One secret can be revealed. We followed the instructions of an infallible guidebook, the Bible. The Person who inspired that Book knows everything about every personality and therefore knows how each should be nurtured.

Even though we tried to follow those instructions, we still made mistakes—many of them—but God overruled our decisions. He made our efforts turn out well. Like kids, we did the best we could with what limited ability we had, but that was not necessarily good enough or wise enough, so like a good father, God stepped in to perfect what we attempted.

One teenage rebel, handed a Bible by his counselor and advised to read a certain verse, became angry and threw the Book at his advisor. "Nobody, and I mean nobody, ain't going to tell me nothin'," he shouted.

Some rebellious parents say the very same thing, except they use better English. The Bible says they are "wise in their own conceits." God has as much trouble with parents who "know it all" as parents do with their "nobody ain't going to tell me nothin'" kids. By contrast, how refreshing it is when a child says, "Dad, I need advice," or a parent says, "God, I need help."

We have learned from experience that God is dependable. When He promises, He keeps His word. What a comfort to discover a promise regarding the raising of children, a promise we could claim with certainty.

In the familiar verse "Train up a child in the way he should go" (Proverbs 22:6) there is also a promise. If we train properly, "when he is old, he will not depart from it." If we keep our part of the bargain, God will fulfill His part.

We noted that the verse specifically says "child." Any training that we intended had to be done while our offspring were young, long before they became adolescents. The Word doesn't say we should train our teenagers or the adults in our household; it says *child*. The earlier we began to teach our children, the easier it would be not only for them but for us as well.

In addition, if they would learn consistent concepts about life and how we wished them to live, we would do the teaching ourselves rather than leaving it to babysitters or nursery school teachers. We had them alone for only five years. After that, the school would influence them as well.

We wanted them to grasp some important teachings—to learn from experience about Jesus Christ so that He would be the central force in their daily lives, not just an appendage tacked on Sunday morning.

We wanted them to experience love—love for God, love for family members, love for those outside the family. And we wanted them to feel secure about our continuous love for them, regardless of what they did or said.

We wanted them to learn obedience. Dr. James Dobson, in his book *Dare to Discipline*, says, "Children thrive best in an atmosphere of genuine love, undergirded by reasonable, consistent discipline." If a child learns to obey his parents, he will also obey God.

We wanted them to be honest in every situation. For telling the truth, no matter what the consequences, they were never punished; for telling lies, they were punished. We wanted them to have a sense of self-worth.

One of the children took a piece of used chalk from the desk in a local furniture store one day. He wanted it for his chalkboard at home. When his father discovered the stolen chalk, he took the child back to the store, where he had to return the chalk to the manager and apologize.

That was not easy for the child or his father. But the experience did teach the child that theft of even a small thing is dishonest and as serious as theft of a more costly item. One of my childhood playmates, who stole carrots from a neighbor's garden, took money from his employer when he was older.

If those patterns were established well while our children were still young, when they became teenagers and wanted to flex their mental and spiritual muscles, they would be capable of doing so.

Dr. Haim Ginott, in his book *Between Parent and Teenager*, says, "No one can mature by blindly obeying his parents." We agree. By the time a person reaches his teens, he should no longer require orders from his parents. Biblical family standards should be so well established by that time that teens are capable of making their own decisions.

They should be given that privilege. When our teens made decisions, we were pleased to discover that such decisions were as prudent as if we had made them ourselves.

While in high school, Curt received a phone call from one of his classmates. "Curt," she began, "I belong to a service club, and we are having our annual ball on Saturday night. I would like you to escort me. Will you?"

"Oh, thanks," Curt responded. "Hold on just a minute, please." Then he asked me, "A girl wants me to take her to a dance. Should I?"

"Do you want to go?" I asked.

"I dunno," Curt replied.

"Tell her you'll call her back," I suggested.

After he hung up the phone, Curt looked to me again for help. "Should I take her, Mom? I don't even know how to dance."

"Well, Curt, you'll have to decide. If after you have thought and prayed about the matter, you believe you should go, then go. If you believe you shouldn't, then tell her so. You have good judgment; you're a Christian. You decide."

After much contemplation, he decided not to go.

In his book *How Christian Parents Face Family Problems*, John C. Wynn says, "Discipline means more than the management of children. It means that they must grow in learning to think for themselves and in ruling themselves."

That "thinking" and "ruling" should begin

while the children are still at home. We should loosen our hold and allow them to decide, even though those decisions are not as we might make them. If they make serious mistakes in judgment, we should be there to cushion their disappointment and help them to begin again.

"Do not deny your teenagers perception," Dr. Ginott says. Let them form their own conclusions based on circumstances as they see them. Teach your children to think for themselves while they are still at home.

We never gave orders to our teens. If the yard needed attention, we might say, "The lawn needs mowing, Skip. Will you have time to do at least some of it after school tonight?"

For other tasks, we might say, "These three things need to be done today. Craig, which one of them will you be able to do?" If one of them had plans that they considered really important, we were flexible and asked them if they could do the particular job at another time.

When our children were approached as adults, they usually reacted in an adult manner. Perhaps that approach was one of the reasons we had no rebels in our household. In any case, we thank God for His goodness.

In our house, we never had curfews. Perhaps strangely, our children never needed them. Although they were active in a number of school, civic, and evening church functions, we never told them when they had to arrive home.

They always came directly home when the activity was finished.

They never just hung around town or fiddled away the night, even though many of their friends did. For some reason, they had the mature sense to come home instead. Teens who display good judgment do not need curfews or adult restrictions.

When our daughter went out with a boyfriend, we would ask, "What time will you be home?" She made that decision. Then we both knew when she would be coming.

Our kids were never grounded for disobedience as many of their friends were. Deliberate disobedience was a rare occurrence. We maintained a friendly relationship with them—an atmosphere of mutual love.

They were as anxious to please us as we were to please them. We were their friends, not enemies, dictators, or fun-spoilers. The term *grounded* was never used in our household for purposes of discipline.

Use of the family car could have been a big problem for us, since we had only one car, but we somehow skirted that dilemma too. None of our teenagers owned a car of his own until the junior year in college, and Jan—who graduated in 1979—still doesn't have one.

While they lived at home, each child was trusted with use of the family car. In all of their growing-up years, only one accident occurred—

a minor one. Craig misjudged the distance between the car and a stone fence and backed into the obstruction. Because he was moving slowly, only a slight dent in the fender resulted.

The fitting of schedules with needs did cause some inconveniences, because more than one person needed the car at times. On such occasions, somebody had to walk. As a result, every member of the family learned to walk without too much complaining, including Mom and Dad.

While teenagers are easing their way from the world of children to the world of adults, they comprise a tantalizing group. Though tantalizing, we discovered that life with them can be sheer pleasure. Though the years were filled with adjustments for all of us, those adjustments helped each one to mature.

Had I known when Skip turned teen just how pleasant the years would be, my fears could have been discarded. Surely I could have been more relaxed and undoubtedly would have enjoyed my teenagers even more than I did.

Our two oldest children, Skip and Craig, suffered the brunt of our fears more than the others. They had to prove to us again and again that they were capable of mature judgment. For a long time we held onto the firmly entrenched view that adolescents in that age bracket are troublesome, and we found it difficult to believe otherwise. They certainly proved us wrong.

By the time Curt turned thirteen, five years after Craig had reached that age, we were relaxed and ready for him. When Janet and Kent became teens, we no longer feared those years. We had learned firsthand how enjoyable children could be in that particular age span. We had also learned that, as they grew older, our bond of love and fellowship with them increased. Instead of growing apart, we moved closer together.

In order to raise such a gratifying quintet, something must have been done right. But we take no credit for that development. God's Word says, "If any of you lack wisdom, let him ask of God, that giveth to all men liberally, and upbraideth not; and it shall be given him" (James 1:5, KJV).*   We simply asked and He gave—typical of our great God.

*King James Version.

Pea Soup Prayers

8

Pea Soup Prayers

Curt taught us about "pea soup prayers."

When he was in grade school, he walked home for lunch every day. As he walked, he would pray something like, "Please, Lord, don't let Mom fix pea soup today."

Why did he pray like that? The answer probably is obvious: he hated pea soup. No matter how hungry he was, a bowl of that "green goop" just didn't appeal to him at all. He knew it was nutritious and good for him, but that did not change his view in the least. Nutritious or not, he wanted no part of pea soup.

This is what I call a "pea soup prayer": it's a prayer in which we acknowledge that we have a problem needing God's help. Instead of allowing

Him to intervene and solve the problem in His own way, however, we tell Him how to provide the solution.

When Curt prayed, he was really saying, "God, I have a need. I'm hungry. Supply that need, but not with pea soup. Give me something I like (apple pie, for instance)." In more concise terms, "This is my need, and this is my solution."

On one hand, in effect, he recognized God's superior abilities, but on the other hand he played the superior role by advising God. Absurd, isn't it? But we are like that.

To refer to my husband's death and my subsequent widowhood as a "pea soup" experience sounds frivolous and lacking in gravity. Nothing is further from the truth. Such an experience is serious business, what psychologists consider perhaps the most devastating blow a person endures. Nevertheless, the term *pea soup* applies here because of its image and ease of recall.

My husband Walt had been having heart problems for some time, with heart surgery twice. Always God answered our pea soup prayers just the way we wanted.

"He is very sick, God, but my five kids and I need him. Please make him well."

God did; that is, until one February night while we were vacationing in Florida. That night, we didn't have time to pray that he might live, for he was dying when we awoke. So instead of praying for life, my sister and I knelt beside him and prayed for victory. What a shock! He went to sleep here with us and woke up in heaven with Christ.

As I look back on the four years that have passed since that event, though filled with the most potentially shattering experiences I have ever had, those years have seen the most spiritual growth in my life during any comparable period. Because my pea soup diet was potent, I was forced to digest some profound spiritual food to survive in good health.

My first "meal" was served in a royal dish engraved with Ephesians 5:20: "Always giving thanks for all things." God, the Master Chef, was telling me I had to thank Him *for* my husband's death if I were going to be spiritually vigorous. I objected.

Like a toddler dumping his pea soup on the floor, I too refused to assimilate that food. Never before had I thanked anybody for anything that did not give me pleasure. Why start now? It just didn't make sense. Though I dumped the whole idea, God did not; that was food I needed to eat—a lesson I needed to learn.

In church, Walt and I had spent many happy hours, most of our time, in fact, outside the home. The church became the most difficult place in the world for me to go alone. Sitting in a pew without him, after having spent more than thirty years by his side, was hard. Every Sunday for weeks I cried. So I began sitting in the balcony, where I would disturb fewer people.

One Sunday I began to cry the moment I entered

the church. Unable to control my tears in spite of all I could do, I decided to walk home. A long walk on such a beautiful June day should be therapeutic. My teens were given the car key.

Although tears continued to fall during the mile-and-a-half walk, God began speaking to me too. In fact, we were having a disagreement concerning His mandate in Ephesians 5:20. "My child," He seemed to say, "you must say thank you for Walt's death."

"But God," I countered, "You don't really mean that, do You? Say thanks *for* his death? What You are telling me is that *in* this dreadful situation I should think of all the good things (nice children, a beautiful day, good health) and thank You for them. That's what You mean, isn't it?"

But the voice persisted. "No, My child. I want you to say thank you *for* your husband's death."

All of a sudden, I felt like a youngster on my daddy's lap and he was telling me, "Now, say thank you to the nice lady for giving you the nice gift." And even though I was too young to appreciate the gift and too immature to understand why I had to say those words, I obeyed His orders, mumbling something that sounded like, "Thank you."

Although I did not understand my father's reasoning any better than I now understood God's, nevertheless I was convinced I had to obey His orders and say my thanks. Neither mandate made sense.

Upon reaching home, I went directly to my bedroom. Kneeling beside my bed, while tears dribbled on the spread, I began to pray.

"God, You know I'm not thankful for my husband's death. I don't know one single thing about it that is pleasant. You've ordered me to say thanks anyway, so here goes. Forgive me for praying a lie; I'm just trying to be obedient."

Attempting to verbalize my thanks, words would not come. After much struggling and weeping, finally I was able to say, "Th-th-th-thanks." Nothing more. Then I rose from my kneeling position.

Dumbest thing I ever did in my life, I thought. *Have to keep it a secret. Mustn't tell my kids—or my friends. Must not be thinking rationally. Probably wind up in Moose Lake* (mental hospital). *Fine testimony that would be.*

For days I pondered, analyzed, and then condemned myself—until I was certain that a complete mental breakdown might be imminent. In search of comfort and help, I continued to read my Bible. One day a shaft of light appeared. It helped me to understand why I was asked to pray such a seemingly strange prayer.

A beautiful revelation clarified the entire confusing episode. I had prayed *in faith*—just like Abraham, Isaac, Moses, and other Bible heroes. In no way comparable to those great Bible characters, I had nevertheless utilized the same principle of faith—on a smaller scale.

In essence, my strange prayer said, "Dear Lord, I don't understand why Walt had to die; why I must

be a widow; why my children must be fatherless.
But I trust You. I have faith in Your judgment,
confidence in Your wisdom.

"If You believe this is best for all of us, then it's all
right with me too. So I thank You, because I trust
You without question."

What blessed relief and release the learning of
that profound truth produced in my life. The
knowledge convinced me that I was not becoming
mentally unbalanced. It was the beginning of healing for my sore, wounded soul—a healing my
friends noticed immediately.

Some said I looked "positively radiant." If that is
true, it reflects only the radiance of Christ who came
to my rescue, and it is because I am happier now
than I ever dreamed I could be—a happiness that
comes from blind obedience to a loving Father.

What the Bible means when it says we should
"glory in tribulations" became clear to me for the
first time. How I praise God for having had the
experience of learning to obey Him by simple
faith—and that most helpful lesson on how to pray
with faith.

One of the most frustrating aspects of being left
without a spouse is the void of not having anyone
with whom to share one's thoughts and inner life.
After years of freely exchanging ideas, hopes, joys,
and sorrows with another, it is extremely difficult
suddenly to be alone.

When something good or bad happened to me or
to someone I knew, my first impulse always had

been, "I must tell Walt." What a jolt to realize he was no longer there to tell. It was like punching a rock. No more vivid way could describe the feeling.

My teens provided marvelous company, but many events and thoughts could not be shared with them. I needed the sympathetic ears of my husband. No one else would do.

What a thrill to discover what God's Word had to say about husbands. "For your husband is your Maker" (Isaiah 54:5). What a revelation! God has promised to be a husband to the widow and a father to the fatherless.

God is my husband, and who on earth can compare with Him? I can go directly to Him with all the frustrations and problems of life, just as before I had gone to Walt. He can take care of me in a way no earthly husband could ever do; He is omnipotent.

Even though God is the ideal husband, the transition from trusting Walt to trusting God did not always prove easy, for I am human. It involved a series of pea soup encounters. Though them all, I learned some valuable lessons.

God has promised to supply every need I have. That means needs without number—physical, mental, emotional, spiritual. So I go to Him often.

"Dear Lord," I pray, "You have promised to care for me, and now I have a biggie that I cannot handle. I'm depending on You to take over. Solve it as You know best." The beauty of it is: He does respond every time—not always as I think He should, but always in a way that is best for me.

There are distinct advantages in trusting God instead of trusting Walt, as I had done for so many years.

For example, God's love is more consistent. Walt's love was conditional, based on his own mood and on my mood. He loved me more when I was lovable and he was in a good mood than he did when I was cross and he was in a bad mood.

God, on the other hand, loves me unconditionally, all of the time, consistently, in spite of my moods. He never changes. Therefore, I am relaxed and cozy in the warmth of a constant, understanding, free-flowing love every single minute. That is a marvelous plus.

Another advantage in shifting my trust from Walt to God is financial. God is far richer! With only the riches of a human husband on which to rely, finances are limited; with God they are limitless.

Walt was extremely generous with the assets he had; God is more generous. With His assets to draw upon, I am potentially a very rich widow. And that is not being facetious; I really am. I have everything I need—happiness, security, and love, resources that even wealthy husbands often are unable to provide for their mates.

Another happy discovery came with a reexamination of Philippians 4:19: "My God shall supply all your needs." God taught me a new facet of that familiar verse. He will supply all of my needs *except* those that I don't want Him to supply.

For example, I sometimes have needs that can evoke sympathy from my friends. If I decide that I would like extra concern from them, I may decide to use that need as a ploy for sympathy. Instead of praying, "Please, God, You take this problem," I hang on to it until I get all the attention I want.

In cases like that, God allows me to wallow in sympathy as long as I choose. Then, when I am sick and tired of wallowing, I give it to Him. Only then, when I am ready, does He take care of that particular need. He never forces His solutions on me.

Sometimes I hang onto a problem or need so that I can use it as an excuse for overindulgence and sin, such as weeping, self-pity, too much food, and so on. Then I may whimper something like, "If you were a widow and had to live alone like I do, you wouldn't be so critical." That excuse is effective in a number of situations because widows (and widowers) do have a host of serious adjustments to make.

God will supply every need and solve every problem that I want Him to solve, but He does not solve those I wish to keep. That much I have learned.

If it is a matter of comparison between God and Walt, it is not difficult to determine who is more capable; God is. But I still miss Walt. Not until I reach heaven do I expect to arrive at the place where I no longer need human companionship.

But I have also learned that when a mate dies, God's grace is sufficient.

There are other hurdles I must overcome as a widow. Presently I am living alone (without even a dog) in the home that at one time housed seven active people. Once a too-busy homemaker trying desperately to keep pace with all the demands my active family placed upon me, now I have few demands except those I place upon myself. How does one cope with such contrasts—such aloneness?

Learning those lessons has been another pea soup set of adjustments—difficult to swallow, but good for me.

Of course, I am not the only widow in the world, nor am I the only lonely person. Millions suffer grief and loneliness, but knowing that doesn't ease my hurting heart. Many lonely days and weepy nights came and went before I learned the secret of happy aloneness. That state of mind, heart, and attitude is attainable.

Not until my husband died and my youngest child left home to attend college did I fully realize how much I had depended on my family for my happiness. Like the hub of a wheel, all of my interests zeroed in on them. What happens to the wheel when the hub is missing? The same thing threatened me; I began to fall apart.

Each day I lived for the telephone calls my kids would make to me, disappointed when none came. Kind friends, realizing my aloneness, called and included me in their activities. Their interest buoyed me up, and I began to depend on them for my happiness.

On weekends and holidays, when they were busy with their spouses and children, I received no attention from them, plunging me into depression. How I longed for Walt and the kids! Beginning to pity myself, I wished I could die too, providing an escape from this sad state of mind. Life was no longer fun.

But that trial also had its purpose. It was a teaching tool to lift me to a higher plane of growth in my spiritual life.

First of all, a new awareness gripped me—the truth that God knew exactly what He was doing when He took my husband. It was no mistake. He knew I would be alone, and lonely. Knowing all that, He allowed it to happen.

Without a doubt, God is good—very, very good, the epitome of goodness. Since that is true, God did not allow those experiences to come into my life to make me miserable, but to make me happy. He allowed them so that I might learn from them.

He wants to perfect me, make me more productive, more loving, more like Christ. He did not allow those things in order to be mean to me; that would be contrary to His very nature. God is love.

With that certain knowledge, why agitate and moan, even in difficult straits? If this is God's will for me, as it surely must be, I must be joyful—by faith. I must acquiesce to His will for my life. I must be willing to be made into His likeness, though it hurts. His wisdom is far better than my own; I must trust Him implicitly.

With those truths firmly embedded in my mind, I sensed a great relief and the desire to get on with living. By nature, I am an introvert. As a protective device, even natural extroverts become introvertive when faced with tragedy. An introvert becomes even more self-centered.

To be happy, I knew that I had to change—to become more of an extrovert. Instead of sitting back and expecting family and friends to make me happy, I must do what I could to make them happy. In making them happy, I would find happiness.

Though contrary to my natural inclinations, I knew it was the only way. As someone has said, "In the happiness of others, I find my own happiness."

God had yet another lesson to teach me: that the hub of my wheel, the focal point of my happiness, had to shift. For so many years, my family had occupied that place; now that they were gone, God must take that position. No doubt, He should have had preeminence all along. Now He could assume His rightful place.

How did that lesson affect my living? Now, instead of depending on my family, their visits, and calls, to maintain a happy state of mind, I look to God. And when family and friends do things to lighten my life, I consider that a bonus.

No longer do I agitate while waiting for a visit

or call that I think surely must come. Now such calls are like exclamation points that add zest to an already happy and fulfilled life—happy because God is the source of my joy, while family and friends are only a secondary source.

"In Thy [God's] presence is fulness of joy; at Thy right hand there are pleasures forever" (Psalm 16:11). I have learned firsthand the reality of that kind of joy.

Yes, my life as a widow has been a severe challenge, with experiences not always enjoyed. Just as I served pea soup to Curt because it was good for him, God allowed those experiences in my life because they were good for me.

Such trials helped me grow up in new areas of my Christian walk. They taught me principles of living I may never have learned had I not become a widow. Having reached a new plateau in my relationship with Jesus Christ, now I can sincerely say, "God, You have allowed this thing to come into my life because I needed it. I still don't like it, because it hurts and hurts badly. But in spite of the pain, thank You, anyway. I still love You."

His help in life's adjustments to self, to family, to others has been invaluable. After all, when it comes to learning how to adjust, God wrote the Book.

Moody Press, a ministry of the Moody Bible Institute, is designed for education, evangelization, and edification. If we may assist you in knowing more about Christ and the Christian life, please write us without obligation: Moody Press, c/o MLM, Chicago, Illinois 60610.